ROAD TRANSPORT IN LONDON

Books LLC®, Wiki Series, Memphis, USA, 2011. ISBN: 9781157615408. www.booksllc.net
Copyright: http://creativecommons.org/licenses/by-sa/3.0/deed.en

Table of Contents

Green Line Coach Station 1
KenBuster 1
London Omnibus Traction Society 1
London congestion charge 2
London low emission zone 11
M4 bus lane 13
Pantechnicon van 15
Smeed Report 15
Streetcar (carsharing) 17
Traffic in Towns 18
Victoria Coach Station 24
Westminster motorcycle parking charge 25

Introduction

Purchase of this book entitles you to a free trial membership in the publisher's book club at www.booksllc.net. (Time limited offer.) Simply enter the barcode number from the back cover onto the membership form. The book club entitles you to select from hundreds of thousands of books at no additional charge. You can also download a digital copy of this and related books to read on the go. Simply enter the title or subject onto the search form to find them.

Each chapter in this book ends with a URL to a hyperlinked online version. Type the URL exactly as it appears. If you change the URL's capitalization it won't work. Use the online version to access related pages, websites, footnotes, tables, color photos, updates. Click the version history tab to see the chapter's contributors. Click the edit link to suggest changes.

A large and diverse editor base collaboratively wrote the book, not a single author. After a long process of discussion and debate, the chapters gradually took on a neutral point of view reached through consensus. Additional editors expanded and contributed to chapters striving to achieve balance and comprehensive coverage. This reduced the regional or cultural bias found in many other books and provided access and breadth on subject matter otherwise little documented.

Green Line Coach Station

Green Line Coach Station is a coach station London, England situated in Bulleid Way, Victoria.

The station offers coach services within Southeast England by Green Line Coaches and Greyhound UK. It should not be confused with the nearby Victoria Coach Station which offers services by National Express Coaches, Megabus and others or with the Victoria bus station which offers urban services from London Buses.
Source (edited): "http://en.wikipedia.org/wiki/Green_Line_Coach_Station"

KenBuster

KenBuster is a GPS-enabled mobile device that will automatically pay the London congestion charge when the vehicle in which it is located enters London's congestion zone. It is intended to avoid paying a heavy penalty resulting from the delayed or neglected payment of the charge. This wireless payment tool was jokingly named after Ken Livingstone, Mayor of London at the time of the congestion zone's introduction.

There are sceptical views about the device's economic sense, due to its high purchase and operating cost compared with the fine for non payment.
Source (edited): "http://en.wikipedia.org/wiki/KenBuster"

London Omnibus Traction Society

The **London Omnibus Traction Society** (LOTS) was formed in 1964 and is the largest society for bus enthusiasts in the UK, dedicated to buses in London and the Home Counties.

The Society produces two main publications:

- *The London Bus* (TLB) has facts, figures and news of the previous month, including route changes, operator news and rolling stock.
- *London Bus Magazine* (LBM), is produced quarterly and has articles, both current and historic, and an 'around and about' section showing pictures of current interest. The magazine is published by Ian Allan.

The Society reports on the central area buses or 'red buses' and country area buses in the previous Green Line area, roughly bounded by Gravesend, Crawley, Guildford, Windsor, Aylesbury, Luton, Harlow and Tilbury.

Among many other publications are the *Bus and Tram fleetbook*, which lists every bus and tram in the London and Home Counties area in public operation.

Details of membership and publications are given on the LOTS website, which is upgraded almost every week with major news stories as well as events and rallies to do with London Buses.

LOTS also has society meetings most months with speakers on different subjects.

Source (edited): "http://en.wikipedia.org/wiki/London_Omnibus_Traction_Society"

London congestion charge

At Old Street, street markings and a sign (inset) with the white-on-red C alert drivers to the charge. The sign displays the original operating hours for the scheme.

The **London congestion charge** is a fee for motorists travelling within the Congestion Charge Zone (CCZ), a traffic area in London. The charge aims to reduce congestion, and raise investment funds for London's transport system. The zone was introduced in central London on 17 February 2003, and extended into parts of west London on 19 February 2007. Though not the first scheme of its kind in the United Kingdom, it was the largest when introduced, and it remains one of the largest in the world. Several cities around the world have referenced London's congestion charge when considering their own schemes.

A payment of £10 is required each day for each vehicle, which travels within the zone between 07:00 and 18:00 (Monday-Friday only); a penalty of between £60 and £180 is levied for non-payment. On 4 January 2011 several changes were implemented based on the public consultation conducted in 2008, which included the removal of the Western Extension, a charge increase from £8 to £10, and the introduction of an automated payment system. Transport for London (TfL) administers the charge; Capita Group operated it under contract until 31 October 2009, and IBM took over on 1 November 2009. The system is mostly run on an automatic basis using Automatic Number Plate Recognition.

Coverage

Area covered by the charge

The boundary of the zone, as of 19 February 2007, starts at the northern end of Vauxhall Bridge and (travelling in a clockwise direction) heads along the northern bank of the River Thames as Grosvenor Road, the Chelsea Embankment and Cheyne Walk. From there, it heads north, along the eastern edges of the Kensington and Earl's Court one-way systems, part of the A3220, with the roads in between charged, before continuing to the A40 Westway as the Holland Road and the West Cross Route. The boundary then includes parts of North Kensington, but the actual boundary is defined by the West London Line railway track, which runs between Latimer Road (inside the zone) and Wood Lane (outside the zone), until Scrubs Lane, before turning east, following the Great Western Main Line out of Paddington towards Ladbroke Grove. Here, the boundary follows the Grand Union Canal and rejoins the existing zone at Edgware Road after skirting Paddington, by way of the Bishop's Bridge Road, Eastbourne Terrace, Praed Street and Sussex Gardens. The Western Extension was officially removed from the charging zone beginning 4 January 2011, but charging on the Western extension effectively ended on 24 December 2010.

TfL has defined some free through routes, where drivers do not have to pay the charge. The main route is defined by the western boundary of the original zone Vauxhall Bridge Road, Grosvenor Place, Park Lane and Edgware Road, with some additions around Victoria. The Westway is the other exempt route.

Original area covered

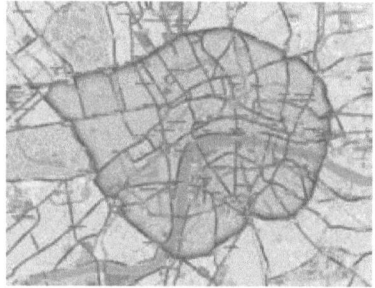

Until 18 February 2007 the congestion charge applied to drivers within the highlighted area.

The original boundary of the zone (17 February 2003 – 18 February 2007) was largely the London Inner Ring Road. Starting at the northernmost point and moving clockwise, the major roads defining the boundary were Pentonville Road, City Road, Old Street, Commercial Street, Mansell Street, Tower Bridge Road, New Kent Road, Elephant and Castle, Vauxhall Bridge Road, Park Lane, Edgware Road, Marylebone Road and Euston Road (other roads filled the small gaps between these roads). The zone therefore included the whole of the City of London, the financial district, and the West End, London's primary commercial and entertainment centre. There were 136,000 residents living within the zone (of a total population of around 7,000,000 in Greater London), though the zone was primarily thought of (and zoned) as commercial rather than residential. There was little heavy industry within the zone. Signs were erected and symbols painted on the road to help drivers recognise the congestion charge area.

Payment and concessions

Payment

As of 4 July 2005, the non-discounted daily charge for non-exempt vehicles is GB£8, or GB£7 for fleet vehicles. Any applicable daily charge must be paid for a vehicle that is driven on a public road in the Congestion Charge Zone between 7 am and 6 pm, Monday to Friday, excluding public holidays in England and the period between Christmas Day and New Year's Day. Drivers may pay the charge online, by SMS text message, in certain shops, or by phone. The charge may be paid the day after travel in the zone at an increased cost of £10.

While drivers of private vehicles can pay the daily charge either the day before, on the day or on the following day, whether they are seen to enter the zone or not, the same does not apply to fleets of business vehicles. Businesses with a minimum of ten or more vehicles can register with TfL, and will be charged GB£7 per vehicle per day for vehicles in the fleet detected by the cameras. In May 2005, businessman Miguel Camacho set up fivepounds.co.uk (referring to the then-current pricing), whose sole function was to sign up private drivers to their "fleet", thus offering the convenience of not having to pay the charge pro-actively, avoiding fines in the case of a forgotten journey and also potentially getting a "free journey" if undetected by the cameras. TfL, which obtains nearly half of its net revenue from fines, moved quickly to quash the loophole, by demanding that fleet operators provide the registration document for each vehicle in their fleet. Fivepounds went out of business on 26 February 2006.

Several changes went into effect beginning 4 January 2011, including the introduction of Congestion Charging Auto Pay (CC Auto Pay), which is an automated payment system that automatically records the number of charging days a vehicle travels within the charging zone each month and takes the charge from a registered debit or credit card on a monthly basis. Any user can nominate up to five vehicles for each CC Auto Pay account and drivers of these vehicles pay a reduced GB£9 daily charge. Those signing up to CC Auto Pay pay an annual £10 registration charge per vehicle. The congestion charges was increased to GB£10 if paid in advance or on the day of travel; to GB£12 if paid by midnight the charging day after travel; and to GB£9 if registered for Congestion Charging Auto Pay.

Exemptions and discounts

Some vehicles such as buses, minibuses (over a certain size), taxis, ambulances, fire engines and police vehicles, motorcycles, very small three-wheelers, alternative fuel vehicles and bicycles are exempt from the charge, although some of the exemptions are 100% discounts that still require registration. Residents of the zone are eligible for a 90% discount if they pay the charge for a week or more at once, although there are administration charges – presently a minimum of £10 – for claiming the discount. Some residents who live close to the West London extension are also entitled to the resident's discount.

Drivers of foreign-registered vehicles are not exempt from the charge but the current lack of an international legal framework for the assessment and collection of traffic fines makes enforcement and recovery difficult. In 2005, *The Guardian* obtained documentation under the Freedom of Information Act 2000 which showed that out of 65,534 penalty tickets issued to non UK registered vehicles, only 1,993 had been paid.

In October 2005, it was reported that two London embassies, those of the United States and Germany, were not paying the charge as they considered it to be a tax, which they are protected from paying under the Vienna Convention. Some other embassies do pay the charge. By May 2006, it was reported, the US embassy owed £270,000 in fines for non-payment. By May 2011, this had risen to £5.5 million. A TfL spokesperson stated that US embassies do pay tolls in Oslo and Singapore. TfL argues that the charge is a toll, not a tax. In April 2006, after not paying it since its introduction in February 2003, the embassy of the United Arab Emirates decided that its diplomats would now pay the charge. As of May 2011, £51m was claimed to be owed to Transport for London by at least ten foreign embassies.

TfL can and does suspend the congestion charge either in a small local area to cope with incidents and if directed to do so by a police officer. The congestion charge was suspended on 7 and 8 July 2005 in response to the terrorist attacks on London Transport. The congestion charge was also suspended on 2 February 2009, in response to an extreme weather event (heavy snow fall) in the London area.

Penalties and avoidance

Failure to pay results in a fine of £120, reduced to £60 if paid within 14 days, but increases to £180 if unpaid after 28 days. Although avoidance has become more sophisticated, compliance with the scheme and terms of payment has improved over the last few years, as is evidenced by the income from penalties dropping by approximately a quarter between 2005 and 2007. However, even after charges were increased, enforcement charges still make up a significant proportion of the net revenues. Several newspapers have reported that copied number plates are being used to avoid the congestion charge, resulting in vehicle owners receiving penalty notices for failure to pay when their vehicles have not been inside the zone. TfL has stated it is keeping a database of these numbers and that they will trigger an alert. The 2008 annual report on the operation of the scheme shows that around 26% of penalties go unpaid, because the notice is cancelled on appeal or the amount cannot be recovered, for example if the registered keeper of the vehicle cannot be traced, is deceased, or bankrupt.

In 2007 a *green motoring website* alleged to TfL that owners of luxury cars were registering their vehicles as minicabs in order to qualify for exemption from the charge. Registering a vehicle as a minicab costs £82 plus £27 per year licence fee, much less than the congestion charge. TfL responded that it carried out regular checks to confirm that cars were being used for the purposes they were registered for, and that they had not discovered any such cases.

Entry authorisation and penalties cannot be issued to non-UK numberplates, and detection cameras may also be unable to read them, meaning that foreign plates are sometimes used to avoid the charge, although cars with foreign plates may only be used in the UK for up to six months before being considered to have been officially imported and thenceforth required to have UK plates.

Operations and technology

Whilst TfL is responsible for the scheme, the operation is sub-contracted to a number of outside companies. Since 2009, IBM is responsible for the day-to-day operation of the charging system, whilst Siemens Traffic Solutions provides and operates the physical enforcement infrastructure. Originally, Capita Group maintained the system under a five-year contract worth around £230m. Having been threatened with the termination of the contract by Ken Livingstone, then Mayor of London, for poor performance, when the zone was subsequently extended, Capita was awarded an extension to the original contract up until February 2009 to cover the expanded zone. Capita has employed sub-contractors including Mastek, based in Mumbai, India, who are responsible for much of the Information Technology infrastructure. Due to the wide spread of sub-contractors around the world and because some data protection regulations vary from country to country, the scheme has prompted concerns about privacy from technology specialists. Transport for London have announced that from 2009 IBM will operate the charge, along with the low emission zone under contract.

The scheme makes use of purpose-built automatic number plate recognition (ANPR) cameras, manufactured by PIPs Technology, to record vehicles entering and exiting the zone. Cameras can record number plates with a 90% accuracy rate through the technology. The majority of vehicles within the zone are captured on camera. The cameras take two still pictures in colour and black and white and use infrared technology to identify the number plates. The camera network and other roadside equipment is managed largely automatically by an instation system developed by Roke Manor Research Ltd, which delivers number plates to the billing system. These identified numbers are checked against the list of payers overnight by computer. In those cases when a number plate has not been recognised then they are checked manually. Those that have paid but have not been seen in the central zone are not refunded, and those that have not paid and are seen are fined. The registered keeper (The registered keeper is presumed to be the owner unless shown otherwise)of such a vehicle is looked up in a database provided by the Driver and Vehicle Licensing Agency (DVLA), based in Swansea.

Road charges

Road tolls

Signs indicate the boundary of the congestion charge area.

Historically, private toll roads, funded by turnpike trusts, were common from the late 17th century until the Local Government Act 1888 passed ownership and responsibility to county and county borough councils. As a result the use of roads in the United Kingdom is generally free of charge, subject to the payment of Vehicle Excise Duty (VED). However, there are specific sections of public roads that remained tolled, which are mainly bridges and tunnels as well as the M6 toll motorway. Of the many previously existing toll roads in London there remains one, College Road in Dulwich, which is privately owned by Dulwich College but accessible by the public.

Road tolls have been advocated by many others in the past, such as the 18th century economist Adam Smith, as a way of directly funding the construction and maintenance of routes.

Road pricing

The government's Smeed Report of 1964 was the first full assessment of the practicality of road pricing in a British city on the basis of congestion. It recommended a method of "car user restraint" by a variable system of charging for road usage – if the government had the will to do so. During the early years of the Greater London Council the first plans were drawn up for a system of cordon charging or supplementary licensing for use in the central area. A formal study was undertaken into the merits of the scheme, and in 1973 concluded that it would improve traffic and environmental conditions in the centre. However, the newly elected Labour council rejected the study's findings in favour of greater investment in public transport. In 1995, the London Congestion Research Programme concluded that the city's economy would benefit from a congestion charge scheme, and the Road Traffic Reduction Act 1997 required local authorities to study and reduce traffic volumes.

The power to introduce "Road user charging" was given to any future mayor in the Greater London Authority Act 1999. Ken Livingstone had proposed in his manifesto to introduce a £5 charge for vehicles entering central London. Following his victory, the Mayor made a draft order and requested a report from TfL, which summarised the reasons for introducing the scheme. The scheme was to be introduced to reduce congestion in the centre of the capital following the *Draft Transport Strategy* of January 2001 which had highlighted the importance that the Mayor placed on tackling this issue. The charge was to be part of a series of measures to improve the transport system in London and was to combined with public transport improvements, increased enforcement of parking and traffic regulations. The report stated that the scheme was expected to be the most effective in reducing through traffic, reducing congestion both within and outside the zone, improving the speed of buses and the quality of life in central London. It was stated that improved traffic flows would make London more attractive to business investment. Substantial net revenues were anticipated, which were to be invested in London's transport system. It also states that 90% of those who responded to a consultation on the scheme, viewed reducing traffic congestion in central London as 'important'.

Having won the first mayoral election in 2000, Ken Livingstone opted to exercise these powers as promised in his independent manifesto, and carried out a series of consultations with interested parties with the basic scheme agreed in February 2002.

Congestion charges in other UK cities

In October 2002, England's first congestion charging scheme was introduced in Durham, it was restricted to a single road in that city, with a £2 charge.

In November 2003, Secretary of State for Transport Alistair Darling said that despite apparent initial interest from many city councils, including those of Leeds, Cardiff, Manchester, Birmingham and Bristol, no city apart from Edinburgh had yet approached the Government for assistance in introducing a charge. Edinburgh City Council proposed a congestion zone, but this was rejected in a postal referendum by around 75% of voters in Edinburgh. Unlike in London, where Ken Livingstone had sufficient devolved powers to introduce the charge on his own authority, other cities would require the confirmation of the Secretary of State for Transport. Manchester proposed a peak time congestion charge scheme which would have been implemented in 2011/2012. This was rejected in a referendum held on 12 December 2008 by over 70% of voters. Plans for similar charges in both the West Midlands and East Midlands have also been rejected. The government has proposed a nationwide scheme of road tolls, but public opposition has been fierce and included a petition of nearly 2 million signatories on the 10 Downing Street website. In an article in the Sunday Times in December 2007, the author describes how he believes that the failure of the London scheme, in terms of value for money, could undermine the Government's desire to convince other parts of the UK to introduce similar schemes.

Congestion charges in other countries

A few other cities around the world already use or have tried congestion pricing schemes, including Singapore (the first scheme in the world, started in 1975, upgraded in 1998), Rome, Valletta, Stockholm, and Milan. Others have implemented a city centre charging zone as a road toll to pay for capital investment in transport infrastructure, including Oslo, Trondheim, and Bergen. A proposal to implement congestion pricing in New York City was stalled in 2008, as the New York State Assembly decided not to vote on it. The congestion charge was one component of New York City Mayor Michael Bloomberg's 'PlaNYC 2030: *A Greener, Greater New York*. San Francisco is the latest American city moving forward with a congestion pricing proposal, which is expected to be implemented as a six-month to one-year trial by 2015.

Effects

The effects of the congestion charge have been controversial. Studies have been made of its effects on congestion, traffic levels, road safety, the use of public transport, the environment, and business activity matters. A report published by TfL in October 2004 stated that only seven of the 13 government aims for London transport would be met by 2010. The target on reducing congestion for Greater London overall will not be met, the report said.

Immediate impact

On the first day 190,000 vehicles moved into or within the zone during charging hours, a decrease of around 25% on normal traffic levels, partly due to it also being the half-term school holiday. A report from the Bow Group stated that historically, London congestion is at its worst during the morning rush hour, and that the early days of congestion charging had little impact on that critical time, the main effect occurring after 11 am. Just over 100,000 motorists paid the charge personally, 15–20,000 were fleet vehicles paying under fleet arrangements, and it was believed around 10,000 liable motorists did not pay the due charge.

Initial suggestions that school holidays were responsible for part of the traffic drop during the first week of operation of the charge were confirmed when traffic rose again by 5% following the return to school at the beginning of the second week of the charge. Reports indicated that, over the first month or so of operation, traffic was consistently down at least 15% on pre-charge levels, with the second week seeing the reduction drop to 20%. The AA Motoring Trust suggested that changes to the timing of traffic lights and the end of major road works had also impacted congestion.

On 23 October 2003 TfL published a report reviewing the first six months of the charge. The report's main findings were that the average number of cars and delivery vehicles entering the central zone was 60,000 fewer than the previous year. Around 50–60% of this reduction was attributed to transfers to public transport, 20–30% to journeys avoiding the zone, 15–25% switching to car share, and the remainder to reduced number of journeys, more traveling outside the hours of operation, and increased use of motorbikes and bicycles. Journey times were found to have been reduced by 14%. Variation in journey time for a particular route repeated on many occasions also decreased. The report also claimed that although the charge was responsible for about 4,000 fewer people visiting the zone daily, that the charge was responsible for only a small fraction of the 7% drop in retail sales reported. The report also stated that around 100,000 penalty fines were issued each month, of which about 2,000 were contested.

By comparison, an experimental short-term congestion charge in Stockholm saw an average 25% reduction in traffic numbers.

Traffic changes

Traffic congestion on the Brompton Road outside Harrods (part of the A4). This road is part of the extended congestion charge zone.

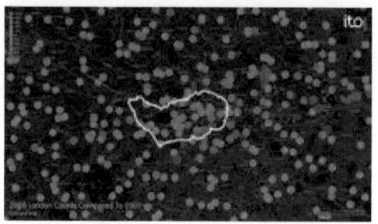

Changes in the counts of cars and taxis in London at October 2008 compared to October 2001. Red dots show a reductions and blue dots increases. The boundary of the congestion charge is shown in white.

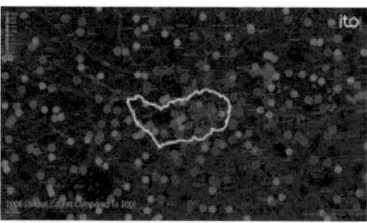

Changes in the counts of bicycles at October 2008 compared to October 2001. Red dots show a reductions and blue dots increases.

A year before the congestion zone, TfL set up automatic traffic counters and augmented them with regular classified traffic counts at key locations, in order to monitor long term trends. Their results are reviewed and reported annually.

A report by TfL in early 2007 indicated that there were 2.27 traffic delays per kilometre in the original charging zone. This compared with a figure of 2.3 before the introduction of the congestion charge. After the scheme was introduced they had measured an improvement in journey times of 0.7 minutes per km, or 30%. This improvement had decreased to 22% in 2006, and during 2006 congestion levels had increased so that the improvement, compared to the year before the scheme, was just 7%. TfL explained this as a result of changes to road priorities within the zone, delays caused by new pedestrian and road user safety schemes, and, most particularly, a doubling of road works in the latter half of 2006. (Utilities were encouraged to complete planned road works in the year proceeding the congestion charge, so it would appear that the first year of measurement used for later comparisons would also have been affected by streetworks to some extent.)

TfL's report in June 2007 found that the level of traffic of all vehicle types entering the central Congestion Charge Zone was now consistently 16% lower in 2006 than the pre-charge levels in 2002. The conservative Bow Group noted that the main effect occurred after 11 am.

Breaking down that figure showed the number of chargeable vehicles entering the zone had reduced by 30% (primarily cars and minicabs, although vans and lorries had decreased by 13%), while there were overall increases in the numbers of taxis, buses, and especially bicycles. The daily profile of traffic flows had changed, with less traffic after 9:30 am and a peak immediately before and after the end of the charging period. The level of traffic entering the zone during the morning peak had not reduced as much as at other times. They had noted a small but pervasive long term trend of less traffic entering the zone, expected to be a result of people changing their location and lifestyle, perhaps influenced by the charge. Once within the charging zone car and delivery traffic remained unchanged, suggesting that the journeys made by residents and businesses within the zone were broadly unaffected. Changes to the road network over the years has made direct comparisons difficult, but TfL suspect that certain routes used heavily by taxis and buses within the zone have seen substantially increased traffic. On some of the boundary roads traffic numbers had increased slightly but congestion and delays were largely unchanged from 2002 levels. Year on year, counts of inbound traffic approaching the zone had also seen a distinct and significant 5–7% decline in the number of chargeable vehicles, which was unexplained.

The charge operates for under one third of the hours in a year and covers around two thirds of the central London traffic. In total 8% of traffic kilometres are affected by the scheme. TfL have extrapolated the trends in road speed in the congestion zone; they have suggested that speeds would have dropped from 17 km/h in 2003 to 11.5 km/h by 2006, had the scheme not been put in place.

Following the introduction of the Western Extension, TfL stated that traffic had fallen around 10 to 15% in the extended zone. The original zone is showing a 4% increase in congestion following expansion of the congestion charge and the introduction of extended to discounts to residents of the new zone and buffer zone. TfL assessed the increase in charges in 2005 to have had only a slight impact overall.

Although it was suggested that the scheme should improve the speed of vehicles in the centre, the London Ambulance Service (LAS) anticipated increased volumes of traffic around the edge of the zone and an increase in demand within the zone, that might both adversely affect clinical outcomes. However, since then, survival rates for LAS' witnessed cardiac arrests have tripled across Greater London. LAS attributes these improvements to equipment availability and operational processes, such as the deployment of four-wheeled and two-wheeled rapid response units that can weave through congestion more quickly. This, and TfL's increase in the number central London traffic calming measures, would suggest that other much more significant factors have masked any congestion charge-related changes in outcome, either up or down. In addition, like some other essential services, LAS felt it necessary to divert about £¼M from their budget to pay congestion charge allowances for key staff affected by the charges during their journey to work.

According to a November 2007 newspaper report, TfL data showed that after an initial improvement, that rush-hour congestion had become worse than it was before the congestion charge was introduced. In December 2007, another article contained a similar observation, that although after the first year the results were looking good, with traffic speeds up, that at the time of writing, traffic speeds and delays were virtually back to their February 2003 levels.

Road safety

TfL have estimated that the charge appeared to have had a small impact on the number of road traffic accidents – but this was much less than the national and London trend towards fewer accidents. There were 2,598 personal injury road traffic accidents inside the zone in the year before the scheme. This fell by about 200 each year to 1,629 in 2005. TfL's statisticians have extrapolated an estimate that between 40 and 70 injuries have been avoided annually because of the charging zone, with most of the rest attributed to the changes that altered and slowed down the road network "in favour of the people-moving capacity of the network."

TfL expects that many of these road safety interventions would have occurred irrespective of the introduction of congestion charging. Cars and motorcycles have seen the biggest reduction in accidents, whereas bicyclists have seen a slight increase, which perhaps reflects their increased numbers. For comparison, the inner ring road also saw a substantial drop as accidents fell from 961 to 632, which was slightly less than the average for Greater London.

Number plate cloning

Another effect of the scheme, which relies on the recognition of vehicle number plates to enforce the charge, is that it has led to an increase in the number of cars carrying false number plates. Fines for non-payment of the charge are sent to the registered keeper of the number plate, without first checking whether the vehicle to which the plate belongs was actually the offending vehicle, the onus being placed on the keeper to prove their innocence. Car breakers are amongst those being targeted as a source for number plates to be illegally used on other vehicles. The BBC reported in October 2005 that the AA Motoring Trust estimated that 1 car in every 250 entering the charging zone was displaying false plates. In 2006 police estimated that more than 40,000 number plate sets were stolen.

Public transport

On the launch date of the original zone, an extra 300 buses (out of a total of around 8,000) were introduced. Bus and London Underground managers reported that buses and tubes were little, if at all, busier than normal. Usage of the Underground has increased by 1% above pre-charge levels, having fallen substantially in 2003/2004, whilst bus patronage in the central London area (not the same as the Congestion Charge Zone) had stabilised at 116,000 journeys per day after increasing from under 90,000 pre-charge. No change in National Rail patronage had been noted as a result of the introduction of the central zone charge.

Since the introduction of the western extension, TfL has made a number of bus route changes to take advantage of the presumed higher traffic speeds and the greater demand for public transport. One new route (route 452) has been introduced and three others (routes 31, 46 and 430) have been extended. In addition, the frequency of buses on other routes through the zone extension has been increased.

Business

The effect of the congestion charge zone on local businesses is a contested issue. The TfL estimates that the effect on business has been overall neutral.

However the effect on business differs significantly by between stores. Some shops and businesses are reported to be heavily affected by the charge, both in terms of lost sales due to reduced traffic and increased delivery costs, as recognised by the London Chamber of Commerce.

The City of London is covered by the congestion charge.

In August 2003, the John Lewis Partnership, a large department store, announced that in the first six months of the charge's operation, sales at their Oxford Street store fell by 7.3% whilst sales at other stores in the Greater London area but outside the Congestion Charge Zone rose by 1.7%. To partly compensate for the loss of revenue they extended opening hours and introduced regular Sunday opening for the first time.

However London First's own report indicated that business was broadly supportive. Subsequently another report stated that there had been a reduction in some employment in the charging zone. TfL criticised the reports as unrepresentative and that its own statistics reported no effect on business.

A report in May 2005 stated that the number of shoppers had declined by 7% year-on-year in March, 8% in April and 11% in the first two weeks of May. TfL countered that an economic downturn, the SARS outbreak and threat of terrorism were likely factors. At the same time a London Chamber of Commerce report indicated that 25% of businesses were planning on relocation following the charges introduction. However an independent report six months after the charge was implemented suggested that businesses were then supporting the charge. London First commissioned the study which reported that 49% of businesses felt the scheme was working and only 16% that it was failing. The Fourth Annual Review by TfL in 2004 indicated that business activity within the charge zone had been higher in both productivity and profitability and that the charge had a "broadly neutral impact" on the London wide economy. The Fifth Annual Review continued to show the central congestion zone outperforming the wider London economy.

The Centre for Economics and Business Research predicted that the West London extension in February 2007 would cause 6,000 job losses. In May 2007, a survey of 150 local businesses stated they had seen an average drop in business of 25% following the introduction of the charge, which was disputed by TfL which stated that there had been "no overall effect" on business and that it had outperformed the rest of the UK in the central zone during 2006.

Environment

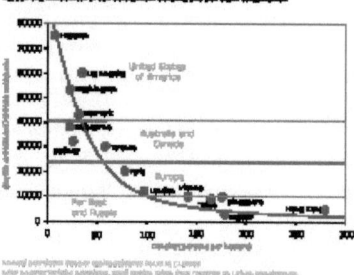

Major cities – per capita petrol use vs. population density

Surface transport accounts for 22% of London's carbon dioxide (CO) emissions. The reduction of airbone emissions wasn't listed as one of the reasons for introducing the congestion charge. The pre-commencement report from TfL noted that the scheme wasn't expected to significantly affect air quality, but that offering a discount to encourage the use of greener fuels would be a positive measure. However, TfL has reported changes in air quality within and alongside the Inner Ring Road boundary of the zone. Levels of two greenhouse gases fell, nitrous oxide (NO), by 13.4% between 2002 & 2003, and carbon dioxide, as well as particulates (PM10). In 2007, the *Fifth Annual Monitoring Report* by TfL stated that between 2003 and 2006, NO emissions fell by 17%, PM10 by 24% and CO by 3%, with some being attributed to the effects of reduced levels of traffic flowing better, with the majority being as a result of improved vehicle technology. In total, the rate of fall in CO has been almost 20% as of 2007. The TfL report makes it clear that only a one-off reduction of emissions could be expected from the introduction of the charge, whilst further reductions are unlikely to be as a result of the charge.

National trends had already shown a rapid decline of some other emissions during the late 1990s, notably carbon monoxide, and levels have been relatively stable since 2002 across London. Since 2002, the nitrogen dioxide (NO) produced by diesel exhaust has become a serious problem, with the London Air Quality Network of King's College London reporting that the annual mean NO objective (of 40 µgm-3 or 21 ppb) was exceeded at all kerbside and roadside monitoring sites across central and greater London during 12 months between 2005 and 2006. Although no areas within the Congestion Charge Zone reported NO levels above an upper limit of 200 µgm-3 (105 ppb), some monitoring areas near the zone boundary experienced very long periods at such levels, notably the A23 near Brixton (3741 hours) and the Marylebone Road (849 hours). TfL report that emissions may not necessarily feed through into improvements in air quality and that vehicle emissions are only one contributor to total emissions of a particular pollutant along with weather conditions and industrial use. It was also reported that pollutant concentrations were being affected by the change in the make up of the vehicle fleet. Preliminary reports also indicate the rate of decline in certain pollutants is decreasing.

A 2011 independent study published by the Health Effects Institute (HEI), and led by a researcher from King's College London, found that there is little evidence the congestion charge scheme has improved air quality. This research used modelling and also compared actual air pollutant measurements within the congestion charge zone with those of control sites located in Outer London. The investigators concluded that "*it is difficult to identify significant air quality improvements from a specific program—especially one targeted at a small area within a large city—against the backdrop of broader regional pollutant and weather changes.*"

Outer London

The charge has proved controversial in the outer areas of London, where it has encouraged commuters who previously drove into central London to instead park at suburban railway or underground stations. This has been accompanied by the introduction of extra on-street parking restrictions and controlled parking zones in these areas, which affects local residents.

Income and costs

TfL's annual report for 2006–7 shows that revenues from the congestion charge were £252.4m over the financial year, representing 8.5% of TfL's annual revenues. More than half of this was spent on the cost of running the toll system, at £130.1 million. Once other charges were deducted, the congestion charge brought in an annual operating net income of £89.1m for TfL. (This income compares with TfL's total revenue from bus and tube fares of £2,269.4m, or 76.6% of revenue before costs, or grants from central government of £2,390.3 million.)

By law, all surpluses raised must be reinvested into London's transport infrastructure; at the start of the scheme it was anticipated that this would be around £200 million. According to a report issued in February 2007, the initial costs of setting up the scheme were £161.7 million, with an annual operating cost of about £115m anticipated. Total revenues over the first three and a half years had been £677.4 million, with TfL reporting a surplus over operating costs of £189.7 million.

The initial operating revenues from the congestion charge did not reach the levels that were originally expected. Within six months of the start of the scheme, the reduction in traffic had been such that TfL were predicting a £65 million revenue shortfall.

The June 2005 increase in charges by 60% only resulted in a relatively small rise in revenues, as there were fewer penalty payments. The anticipated start up costs of the Western extension were £125 million with operating costs of £33m; expected gross revenues were expected to be £80 million resulting in net revenues of £50 million.

Although Parliament has limited the amount that authorities can borrow, for some time it had been speculated that the regular income obtained from the congestion charge and other revenues could be used to securitise a bond issue that finances other transport projects across London. TfL issued their first bond for £200 million in 2005, to be repaid at 5% interest over 30 years. TfL plans to borrow £3.1 billion more to fund a 5-year transport programme across London, including works on London Underground and road safety schemes.

Political reaction

Before the charge's introduction, there were fears of a very chaotic few days as the charge bedded down. Indeed Ken Livingstone, then Mayor of London and key proponent of the charge, himself predicted a "difficult few days" and a "bloody day".

In July 2002, Westminster City Council launched a legal challenge against the plans, arguing that they would increase pollution and were a breach of human rights of residents on the boundary of the zone. The High Court rejected the claim. On introduction, the scheme was the largest ever undertaken by a capital city.

Steven Norris, the Conservative Party candidate for mayor in 2004, has been a fierce critic of the charge, branding it the 'Kengestion' charge. A few days before the scheme came into operation, he wrote in a BBC report that it had been "shambolically organised", that the public transport network had insufficient spare capacity to cater for travellers deterred from using their cars in the area by the charge. Further, he said that the scheme would affect poorer sections of society more than the rich, with the daily charge being the same for all, regardless of vehicle size. He pledged to scrap it if he became mayor in June 2004. He had also pledged that, if elected, he would grant an amnesty to anyone with an outstanding fine for non-payment of the charge on 11 June 2004. In an interview with London's *Evening Standard* newspaper on 5 February 2004, Conservative leader Michael Howard backed his candidate's view by saying that the charge "has undoubtedly had a damaging effect on business in London." Liberal Democrat candidate, Simon Hughes, however, supported the basic principles of the scheme. Amongst some of the changes he proposed were changing the end time from 6:30 pm to 5 pm and automatically giving all vehicles five free days each year so as not to affect occasional visitors.

In 2005, the Liberal Democrats claimed that Capita had been fined £4.5 million for missing the targets set for the congestion charge, that was equivalent to £7,400 for every day that the charge had existed. The *London Assembly Budget Committee* 2003 report on the company criticised the contract with Capita as not providing value for money. It was reported in July 2003 that TfL agreed to subsidise Capita by paying it £31 million because it was making no profits from the project, and that the most critical problem was the 103,000 outstanding penalty notices not paid. Capita was also the company that won the 'Most Invasive Company' award in the Privacy International 2003 Big Brother Awards.

Congestion charge CCTV cameras on Vauxhall Bridge Road

The congestion charge remained an issue during the run up to the 2008 mayoral election. Boris Johnson, the Conservative Party candidate suggested looking at a graduated charging scheme and proposed further consultation on whether to remove parts of the Congestion Charge Scheme. He also said that he would not introduce the emissions based charging system which was due to be introduced in October 2008

Brian Paddick, the Liberal Democrat candidate, suggested exempting delivery vehicles from the charge.

The successful mayoral candidate Boris Johnson announced on 8 July 2008 that his predecessor Ken Livingstone's plan to introduce a £25 charge for the heavy-polluting vehicles will not go ahead.

Further proposals

After the introduction of the charge, there were a number of suggestions for its future. Soon after charging commenced, Livingstone announced that he would carry out a formal review of the charge's success or failure six months after its introduction – brought forward from one year, following the smooth start. On 25 February 2003 Livingstone stated, "I can't conceive of any circumstances in the foreseeable future where we would want to change the charge, although perhaps ten years down the line it may be necessary" referring to the amount that drivers have to pay, indicating that £5 was sufficient to bring about the reduction in traffic that he had hoped for. By November 2004, Livingstone directly contradicted his earlier stance and said in an interview with BBC London, "I have always said that during this term [his second term in office] it will go up to at least £6." By the end of the month, Livingstone changed his position again, saying in an announcement that, in fact, the rise would be to £8 for private vehicles and £7 for commercial traffic. Business groups such as London First said following the announcement that the charges were "totally unsatisfactory and unacceptable". The rise to £8 was announced formally on 1 April 2005, along with discounts for drivers buying month or year-long tickets. On 10 May 2006, in a live TV debate, Livingstone supported a rise in the charge to £10 by 2008.

Western extension

Park Lane is one of the new free through routes.

In February 2004, TfL issued a consultation document on the expansion of the zone to the west that would cover the rest (western portion) of Westminster and the Royal Borough of Kensington and Chelsea. The extension covered around 230,000 residents, compared with the 150,000 in the original zone.

In August 2004, following Livingstone's re-election in the June 2004 mayoral election, the results of the consultation were published. A substantial majority of respondents did not want the extension, however Livingstone said he was going ahead and that the polls were a "charade" which did not diminish his electoral mandate. "A consultation is not a referendum" he said. Protests continued against the extension, with residents arguing that only 5% of the road space in the selected area was congested. Following on in May 2005 TfL a further consultation began with specific proposals about the extensions. These included a plan to reduce the operating hours of the charge by half-an-hour to "boost trade at London's theatres, restaurants and cinemas".

At the end of September 2005, London Mayor Ken Livingstone confirmed the western expansion of the congestion charge, which came into effect on 19 February 2007. It was expected that the extension would increase congestion in the zone by around 5% as the 60,000 residents in the new zone will be entitled to the discounts available. Several roads were also to be left charge-free between the original zone and the extension.

However, the current Mayor of London, Boris Johnson, at the beginning of his administration, announced that he would discard plans for extending the charge zone to the suburbs, and also announced he will review the western extension implemented in 2007, based on a public consultation planned for September 2008. Having held a five-week public consultation with residents in autumn 2008, Johnson agreed to remove the western extension of the congestion charging zone by 2010. Out of 28,000 people who responded to the consultation, 67% of the respondents, including 86% of businesses, said they wanted the extended zone removed.

On 20 October 2010, TfL announced that Mayor Johnson decided to remove the Western Extension which, together with other changes to the scheme, were scheduled to take effect from 4 January 2011. However, because there is no charging due to the Christmas holidays, charging on the Western extension effectively ended on 24 December 2010.

Transponder charging

TfL ran a six month trial of "tag and beacon" (transponder) from February 2006 to replace the camera based system. This uses an electronic card affixed to the windscreen of a vehicle and can be used to produce "smart tolls" where charges can be varied dependent on time and direction of travel. This system automatically deducts the charge so that the 50,000 drivers a year who forget to pay the fine would not be penalised. TfL has suggested that this scheme could be introduced from 2009.

Blackwall Tunnel charging

Transport for London consulted on a charge for the Blackwall Tunnel in east London, but these proposals have been suspended following significant opposition from the public. Former Mayor Ken Livingstone has stated that he had "absolutely no plans to set up a congestion charging zone to charge vehicles that use the Blackwall Tunnel or the Blackwall Tunnel Approach Road. But if Greenwich wishes to do so on any of its roads then I will support them".

Emissions based fee structure

A new emissions-based fee structure was proposed by mayor Ken Livingstone in 2006. It would have charged more for drivers in higher CO emission rate Vehicle Excise Duty bands. The change was due to start in October 2008, but the new Mayor Johnson announced on 8 July 2008 that the new CO charging structure will no longer be implemented. Among other reasons, he said the environmental charge would encourage travel by thousands of smaller vehicles for free, resulting in increase congestion and pollution.

History

The proposal was put forward the end of 2006 by Ken Livingstone; a variable congestion charge based on the Vehicle Excise Duty (VED) bands would be introduced. This would reduce or eliminate the charge for *Band A* vehicles, and increase it to up to £25 a day for *Band G* vehicles, with CO emissions greater than 225 g/km.

Consultation on these proposals began in August 2007 and ended on 19 October 2007.

On 12 February 2008 TfL announced that on 27 October 2008 they would introduce a new charging structure for vehicles entering the congestion zone, based on potential CO emission rates.

The main change would be the introduction of two new fees:

- £25 per day (with no residents' discount) for *cars* which, if first registered on or after 1 March 2001 are rated in Vehicle Excise Duty (VED) "Band G" (emitting above 225g/km of CO), or if first registered before 1 March 2001 have an engine capacity of greater than 3000 cc and for *pickups* with two rows of seats which either are rated as emitting above 225g/km of CO or which have an engine capacity of greater than 3000 cc. It should be noted that in Alistair Darling's 2008 budget it was announced that VED Band G would be lowered to 151g/km of CO. TfL had not clarified whether the £25 daily charge would be linked to the band until the point became moot as the scheme was cancelled.

- £0 per day (a 100% discount) for cars that either are rated as emitting less than 120g/km CO and which meet the Euro 4 air pollution emissions standard or which are rated as emitting no more than 120g/km CO and which appear on the PowerShift register.

Acting director of the RAC Sheila Raingner stated that "The congestion charge was originally developed to reduce congestion. Changing this will confuse the public and reduce support and trust for future initiatives."

Land Rover commissioned a report from the Centre for Economics and Business Research think tank, which concluded that the scheme would increase pollution. It had also been criticised by car manufacturer Porsche, who announced they intended to request a judicial review. They claimed that the new charges were disproportionately high, and would not make a 'meaningful difference' to the environment.

At the request of Porsche, King's College released the full report of the possible effects of the new system that was originally commissioned by Transport for London. This report indicated that the proposed new system would reduce CO emissions in central London by 2,200 tonnes by 2012, but would increase CO emissions by 182,000 tonnes in outer London, due to drivers of more polluting vehicles avoiding congestion charge zones.

Upon the release of this report, a spokesman Transport for London stated that the methodology used by King's was 'less robust and accurate than TfL's methodology'. They stated that their findings suggested reductions of up to 5000 tonnes of CO by 2009, and claimed that King's College agreed with these results and were making revisions to their report.

Source (edited): "http://en.wikipedia.org/wiki/London_congestion_charge"

London low emission zone

The **London Low Emission Zone** (LEZ) is a charging scheme with the aim of reducing the pollution emissions of diesel-powered commercial vehicles in London, England. Vehicles are defined by their emissions and those that exceed pre-determined levels are charged to enter Greater London. The low emission zone started operating on 4 February 2008. There is a planned phased introduction of an increasingly stricter regime up to 2012, when it will be fully operational. The scheme is administered by the Transport for London executive agency within the Greater London Authority.

Background

Signage at entrance to low emission zone

Airborne pollution in London is the worst in the United Kingdom, and amongst the worst in Europe, and roadside pollution has been rising for two years. A Green Party report stated that in 2007, nine sites in London exceed the EU limits for air pollution, in 2000 it was only one. Since 1993 the London Air Quality Network of King's College London has co-ordinated the monitoring of air pollution across 30 London boroughs and Heathrow, and has noted that in 2005-6 almost all road and curbside monitoring sites across greater London exceeded the annual average limits for nitrogen dioxide of 40 µgm-3 (21 ppb), with eleven sites exceeding the hourly limits of 200 µgm-3 (105 ppb) on at least 18 occasions each. (The A23 at Brixton suffered the most consistently high levels for more than two-fifths of the period.) This compares to 2002 when only one site exceeded these limits. They also note that carbon monoxide levels reduced rapidly during the late 1990s and have been relatively stable since 2002.

72% of the population is concerned about air quality. Transport for London (TfL) has stated that there are an estimated 1,000 premature deaths and a further 1,000 hospital admissions annually, due to poor air quality from all causes.

Towards the end of 2006, the Mayor of London Ken Livingstone proposed changing the congestion charge fee, from being a flat rate for all qualifying vehicles, to being based on Vehicle Excise Duty (VED) bands. VED bands for new vehicles are based on the results of a laboratory test, designed to calculate the theoretical potential emissions of the vehicle in grammes of CO per kilometre travelled, under ideal conditions. The resulting figures, described as "deeply flawed" by the editor-in-chief of *What Car?* magazine, are then used to define the band in which a particular vehicle falls. The lowest band, *Band A*, is for vehicles with a calculated CO value of up to 100 g/km, the highest band, *Band G*, is for vehicles with a CO value of greater than 225 g/km. Under the proposed modifications to the scheme, vehicles falling into *Band A* would have a reduced, or even zero charge, whilst those in *Band G* would be charged at £25 per day. Certain categories of vehicle, including electric vehicles, are already exempt from the charge. These proposals were put out to public consultation in August 2007.

In early 2006, consultations began on another charging scheme for motor vehicles entering London. Under this new scheme, a daily charge would be applied to the vehicles responsible for most of London's road traffic emissions, commercial vehicles – such as lorries, buses and coaches, with diesel engines. Cars were explicitly excluded. The objective of the new scheme is to help London meet its European Union (EU) air pollution obligations - specifically the EU Air Quality Framework Directive - as part of the Mayor's programme to make London the greenest city in the world. Despite some opposition, on 9 May 2007 the Mayor confirmed that he would proceed with a London Low Emission Zone, focused entirely on vehicle emissions, that plans to reduce emissions overall by 16% by 2012.

Scheme

Outline of Greater London. The LEZ covers most of this area

The LEZ came into operation on 4 February 2008 covering most of Greater London, though in some places the zone deviates to allow diversionary routes and facilities to turn around without entering the zone. The M25 motorway is not included in the scheme where it enters Greater London for short stretches in the west, north and east. Signage indicates the boundaries of the zone which operates 24 hours a day, 7 days a week, the largest such zone in the world. There will be a phased introduction of further provisions through to January 2012. Different vehicles will be affected over time and increasingly tougher emissions standards will apply. The scheme applies to diesel engine vehicles over 1.205 tonnes which must be registered with TfL. The scheme does not affect cars or motorcycles. Owners of vehicles that do not meet these requirements must pay a fee of £200 with failure to pay resulting in a fine of up to £1,500. A limited range of vehicles are exempted or able to obtain a discount from the charge. Payment of the LEZ charge is in addition to any congestion charge required.

Vehicles registered after October 2001 will generally be compliant with the first stages of the zone as from this date Euro 3 engine compliance was a mandatory requirement. Specific engines registered before October 2001 may also be compliant. Vehicles not specifically listed can be registered with TfL subject their owners obtaining a Low Emission Certificate (LEC) from the Vehicle and Operator Services Agency (VOSA) subject to passing a supplementary smoke test or for non UK vehicles a specified operator certificate. Most vehicles do not need to be registered as TfL has compiled a list of compliant vehicles from information held by Driver and Vehicle Licensing Agency (DVLA), VOSA and the Society of Motor Manufacturers and Traders.

Like the congestion charge, the zone is monitored using Automatic Number Plate Reading Cameras (ANPR) to record number plates. Vehicles entering or moving around the zone are checked against the records of the DVLA to enable TfL to pursue owners of vehicles for which the charge has not been paid. For vehicles registered outside of Great Britain, an international debt recovery agency is used to obtain unpaid charges and fines. The scheme is operated on a day-to-day basis by IBM.

Reaction

The scheme was opposed during the consultation phase by a range of stake holders. The Freight Transport Association proposed an alternative scheme, reliant on a replacement cycle of vehicles, with lorries over 8 years old being liable, with higher years for other vehicles. They also stated that the standards were different than the forthcoming Euro 5 requirements as well suggesting the scheme did not do anything to help reduce CO_2 emissions. The Road Haulage Association opposed the scheme, stating the costs to hauliers and benefits to the environment did not justify its introduction.

Schools and St. John Ambulance have expressed concern about the additional costs that the scheme will bring them, particularly in light of the restricted budgets they operate under.

The proposals were welcomed by the British Lung Foundation and the British Heart Foundation. London First, a business organisation, criticised aspects of the scheme with relation to the categorisation of vehicles, but supported the principle.

Changes to Phase 3 - proposed suspension of 2010 implementation

On 2 February 2009 the Mayor of London, Boris Johnson, announced his intention to cancel the third phase of the LEZ covering vans from 2010, subject to the outcome of a public consultation later in the year. The Freight Transport Association welcomed this move in its press release of 3 February.

Source (edited): "http://en.wikipedia.org/wiki/London_low_emission_zone"

M4 bus lane

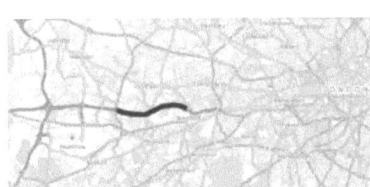

Map showing location of the bus lane

M4 bus lane near Norwood Green, Ealing

The **M4 bus lane** was a controversial 3.5-mile (5.6 km) bus lane on the eastbound (London-bound) carriageway of the M4 motorway between Heathrow Airport and central London. It operated between junction 3 (A312) to the start of the elevated 2-lane section near Brentford. The lane, which had no intermediate junctions, was reserved for buses, coaches, motorbikes, emergency vehicles and licensed taxis but not minicabs.

The lane opened as a pilot in June 1999 and was made permanent in 2001. It was suspended during December 2010 using an 18 month Experimental Traffic Order after which it will be reinstated temporarily for the 2012 London Olympics. It is then likely to be scrapped permanently.

History

The lane, replacing the original offside lane (the lane nearest to the central reservation) of the motorway, was opened as a pilot by the then Deputy Prime Minister, John Prescott on 7th June 1999 and was made permanent in 2001. A speed limit of 50 mph was created when the bus lane opened, which was then raised to 60 mph in 2003 when motorcycles were also allowed to use the lane.

Research into the effect of the lane was undertaken by the Transport Research Laboratory in 2000 and 2003.(see below)

On 1 October 2010 it was reported that the transport secretary, Philip Hammond, was likely to announce at the conservative party conference that the lane would be suspended for 18 months from 24 December 2010 to be brought back for the 2012 Summer Olympics after which it would be scrapped.

A Whitehall source was quoted as saying that the business-case for removing the bus-lane showed time savings for all current non-bus lane users during the morning peak period and evening peak with no significant change in journey times for existing bus lane users'. During his speech to the Conservative Party conference Philip Hammond explained that removing the bus lane would result in 'shortening average journey times; reducing congestion; restoring a sense of fairness. Seven Freedom of information requests were made the following day to various organisations (see below).

A section of the bus lane was removed and the lane reverted to all-traffic use on 16 November 2010. By the end of December 2010 the entire lane had been removed and the full road width reverted back to all-traffic use.

Usage

In addition to taxicabs and motorcycles, a number of UK coach services also use the lane. National Express Coaches services include: 030/032 (Portsmouth-London), 033 (Salisbury-London), 035 (Poole-London), 040 (Bristol-London), 402 (Frome-London), 403 (Bath-London), 404/504 (Penzance-London), 413 (Hereford-London), 421 (Blackpool-London), 501 (Totnes-London), 502 (Westward Ho!-London), 505 (Newquay-London), 508 (Haverfordwest-London), 509 (Swansea-London) and 509 (Aberdeen-London); Megabus operate M14 (Cheltenham-London), Green Line Coaches operate their 701 and 702 (Bracknell-London) service and Berry's Coaches the 351 (Tiverton-London) service.

In May 2001 a Sunday Times survey found that of 111 buses that used the bus lane over a 5 hours 50 minute period, 38 were carrying no passengers, 37 were carrying 10 or fewer passengers, 15 were half full and 21 were full.

Research

A study by the Transport Research Laboratory 'Monitoring of the M4 bus lane: the first year' was produced in 2000 reported that the £1.9m scheme had reduced rush hour journey times by 3.5 minutes for buses and one minute for cars. Off-peak car journey times were a minute longer due to a reduced speed limit which was cut from 70 miles per hour (110 km/h) to 50 miles per hour (80 km/h) and overall journey times had increased by 1.8%. CO_2 emissions were cut by 16%, fuel consumption had improved by 16% and that noise levels were down by one decibel.

Transport for London reported that the 7% of M4 traffic that used the bus lane carried 21% of the people.

TRL produced a further report in 2003 'Monitoring of the M4 bus lane: 2000 to 2002'.

A 2005 literature review of research into high-occupancy lanes produced for the Highways Agency reported that the lane was used about 3700 vehicles a day (3100 taxis, 500 buses or coaches and 100 minibuses) and that there was an overall benefit was 200 person-hours per weekday and a dis-benefit of 350 person-hours per weekend day; the dis-benefit being the result of the reduced speed-limit.

A number of freedom on information requests have been made in relation to the M4 bus lane.

14 August 2009 Highways Agency which revealed that a total of 20 Penalty Charge Notices had been issued since January 2008 for misuse of the bus lane.

29 October 2009 Public Carriage Office Bus Lane which revealed that 192 complaints had been made about private hire vehicles using the bus lane.

Seven FOI requests were received agencies on the 2 October 2010 following the announcement that the lane was to be removed. Two were to the Highways Agency. The first requested details of data held relating to the operation of the bus lane, in particular reports produced by the Transport Research Laboratory and around the decision to remove the lane. The Response delayed due to the "The complexity and volume of the requested information and the current position surrounding the issues of the M4 bus lane mean that it is impracticable for us to give a full response within the original 20 days". The second requested details of the changes, communications relating to the changes and analysis.

On the same day a request was sent to the Department for Transport requesting details of data held and correspondence relating to the bus lane. No response had been received by 13 November 2010. A request was also sent to the Transport for London. They responded saying that they had not been part of any discussion. Similarly Hillingdon Borough Council,, Ealing Borough Council, and Hounslow Borough Council responded saying that they had not been part of any discussion. A request was sent to the Prime Minister's Office on 13 October 2010 requesting details of consultation regarding the removal of the M4 Bus Lane. No response had been received by 13 November 2010.

Controversy

The lane has been controversial since it was first introduced; In 2001 the Automobile Association suggested that it could only be deemed a success if 'significant numbers of drivers switched from their cars to public transport' and Jeremy Clarkson of *Top Gear* said he would 'vote for anyone who promised to tear up that stupid pinko bus lane'. When John Prescott appeared as a guest on *Top Gear* on 27 February 2011, the bus lane was the first topic raised by Clarkson. Citing independent research, Prescott maintained that reducing the motorway to two general lanes, had improved traffic flow and raised the average speed and lowered journey times for all users, while also improving safety. Countering this theory, Clarkson asked why the government had agreed to widen other motorways, which Prescott justified on the rise in number of cars on the roads (7 million new cars).

In 2009 the Automobile Association described it as an underused 'white elephant'. When announcing the suspension of the scheme in 2010 Philip Hammond said that 'Nothing is more symbolic of Labour's war on the motorist', the RAC Foundation supported the move with director Stephen Glaister commenting that 'Most drivers on the M4 will wonder why this decision has taken so long'. *The Sun* described the bus lane as 'insane'. A Freedom of Information request in 2009 revealed that the bus lane was barely enforced, with only 20 fixed penalty notices being issued in the preceding 18 months and that private drivers able to get away with regularly driving in it.

Source (edited): "http://en.wikipedia.org/wiki/M4_bus_lane"

Pantechnicon van

This article is about the horse-drawn vehicle. For the modern equivalent, see pantechnicon.

A **Pantechnicon van**, currently usually shortened to **pantechnicon**, was originally a furniture removal van drawn by horses and used by the British company "The Pantechnicon" for delivering and collecting furniture which its customers wished to store. The name is a word largely of British English usage.

Origins

The word Pantechnicon is an invented one, formed from the Greek *pan* ("all") and *techne* ("art"). It was originally the name of a large establishment in Motcomb Street, Belgrave Square, London, opened around 1830. It combined a picture gallery, a furniture shop, and the sale of carriages, while its southern half was a sizable warehouse for storing furniture and other items. The Seth Smith brothers, originally from Wiltshire, were builders in the early 19th century and constructed much of the new housing in Belgravia, then a country area. Their clients required storage facilities and this was built with a Greek style Doric column façade, and called Pantechnicon, Greek for "pertaining to all the arts or crafts". Subsequently special wagons were designed with sloping ramps to more easily load furniture with the building name on the side.

The very large, distinctive and noticeable horse-drawn vans which were used to collect and deliver the customers' furniture came to be known as Pantechnicon vans. The warehouse itself was destroyed by fire in 1876 but the usefulness of the vans was by then well established and they had been adopted by other firms. From around 1900, the name was shortened to simply Pantechnicon.

The Pantechnicon Ltd, a furniture storage and removal company continued to trade until the 1970s. The building was largely destroyed by fire in 1874, but the facade still exists as part of an antique shop.

Design

Though small by modern standards, they were impressively large by those of their own time. They came in lengths of between 12 and 18 feet, were up to 7 feet broad. The roof was a segment of a cylinder 8 inches higher in the middle than at the edges to ensure ready drainage but it had boards round the edges to allow stowage of extra items. Below the roof-line the body was a cuboid box except that behind the space required by the front wheels when turning tightly, the floor was lowered to permit greater internal headroom. This was achieved by cranking the back axle downwards as in a float. The lowered floor also saved some of the lifting which was a feature of using normal horse-drawn lorries and vans, which needed a deck high enough to fit the steering mechanism below it. Access was obtained through hinged doors at the rear. Outside these, the tailboard was hinged upwards from the level of the well.

Use

They were drawn by two horses in tandem. This seems to have been so as to allow entry to relatively narrow town lanes and such places as the warehouse doorways. To give the driver a clear view of obstructions and to enable him to control the lead horse, he was usually seated on the front of the roof.

The value of these vans seems to have been quite quickly appreciated so that removal firms other than The Pantechnicon operated them, sometimes over long distances between towns. This business was fairly soon made easier however, as the railways did this part of the work more quickly. This is probably where the carefully limited dimensions really arose. The railways had strict rules about loading gauges and the vans were carried between towns, tied down to platform trucks. Take away the coaming boards from around the roof; remove the shafts, fold up and stow the traces and you were left with something remarkably like a British railway goods van, a boxcar

So the pantechnicon van was an early example of ro-ro, capable of taking furniture from door to door. This is not at all surprising. The London and Greenwich Railway set out from its opening in 1836, with the idea of starting passengers on their way along the Dover Road by carrying them in their own carriages chained down to flat bed trucks with their horses carried in a van (boxcar).

Modern usage

A pantech truck or van is a word derivation of "pantechnicon" commonly currently used in Australia. A pantech is a truck or van with a freight hull made of (or converted to) hard panels. Such vehicles can be used for chilled freight, or as removal vans. The articulated lorries used by the British removals company Pickfords & Son were referred to in the jargon of the day as "articulated pantechnicons".

Source (edited): "http://en.wikipedia.org/wiki/Pantechnicon_van"

Smeed Report

The **Smeed Report** was a study into alternative methods of charging for road use, commissioned by the UK government between 1962 and 1964. The report stopped short of an unqualified recommendation for road pricing but concluded that it could work and should be considered for congested road networks.

It was named after R. J. Smeed, the deputy director of the British Transport and Road Research Laboratory, who headed the team that studied the feasibility of charging motorists for using congested road networks.

The report was written by a body of 11 economists and engineers, including Michael Edwin Beesley, a pioneer of Cost Benefit Analysis techniques whose key innovation was the valuation that people give to their time, and Gabriel Roth, a noted road transport economist. Smeed was also a noted statistician and transport planner: he identified Smeed's law that describes motorists' tolerance towards speed and risk. He observed that drivers would not go out if traffic speeds fell below 9 mph; but if speeds rose, more would drive until they caused more congestion.

The report suggested alternatives to the system of road taxation and user benefits that was in use at the time and was based largely on the results of the 1933 Salter Report into road and rail transportation.

Conclusions

The results of the revolutionary study were reported into the then Ministry of Transport, indicating that the effect of speeding up congested traffic would benefit the country's economy by £100-£150M per annum. It would be possible and feasible to impose car user restraint strategies by charging through the metering of road usage, *if the government had the will to do so.*

The principles laid down were that "The road user should pay the costs that he imposes upon others", namely the following:
- road costs (construction, maintenance, lighting)
- congestion (the delay the motorist causes to others)
- social costs (risk, noise, fumes)

The operational requirements should be the following:
- related to the amount of use made of the roads
- costs should vary according to the location, time, and type of vehicle
- cities should be zoned, with costs raising to 10 shillings per hour of driving in the centre of London or Cambridge
- costs should be stable and known in advance
- payment in advance of travel should be possible

Charging zones would be identified by clear signs on their boundaries; these could be electrical and thus be changed at various times of the day. A simple national colour-coded scheme could be used to indicate the charge rate in force at that time or to allow different charging zones to exist side-by side.

They recognised that traditional toll collection methods would not be practical in city centres, where the road layout had not been designed to provide natural gateways into the tow, and where the demolition and land required for toll booths or toll plazas would be unacceptable.

Instead, they investigated charging through a daily licence system, managed either by a remote wireless automatic identification of the vehicle, or by a meter mounted inside the vehicle, which could track both driving charges and parking.

They recommended a tamper-proof credit or pre-payment meter inside the car, as with the technology available at the time, any external recording mechanism would require expensive equipment for tracking and book keeping and threaten the privacy of the vehicle users they tracked. A single metering system could be used in any British city centre that chose to adopt a charging zones.

There was also an economic analysis that showed that the largest part of the economic benefit from road pricing was not in the relief of congestion but in the revenue collected, which would only be released when the revenue is used. In the arguments that followed, the good that could come about by using the money from such a scheme was frequently overshadowed by a vision of the restraints and penalties levied on the motorist.

Reactions

The report was received with ambivalence by the Macmillan government, which had commissioned it: the Ministry reported in June 1964 that it would first need to study the implications and thus the government was "therefore in no way committed to this form of restraint". It initially withheld release of the full report to the public and took its time to consider it. It was rumoured that the Prime Minister, Sir Alec Douglas Home, had suggested to "take a vow that if we are re-elected we will never again set up a study like this one".

Events took over, and two elections were fought in 1964 and 1966 with transport as a major election issue, resulting in a new Wilson government with Barbara Castle as Minister of Transport. A large majority enabled her to bring into law a number of the then-controversial safety concepts that the RRL had been investigating, such as speed limits and breathalyzers. She appeared to become an advocate of road pricing per the Smeed Report and publicly criticised the construction of new urban motorways as "self-defeating", during a tour of US cities, slowing down the UK's future urban road building programme as a consequence.

However, the political will needed to establish such a scheme seemed to be slipping away, and commitment atrophied in the UK as the minister requested more feasibility reports, until, in 1970, the government changed and the scheme effectively died.

The Smeed committee members had already become frustrated and moved on. In 1966, Smeed was appointed Professor of Traffic Studies at University College London (UCL) and formed the then Research Group in Traffic Studies, which grew to become the present Centre for Transport Studies at UCL within the University of London Centre for Transport Studies. The chair of the parallel and quasi-competing committee, Professor Sir Colin Buchanan took up a post as professor of transport at Imperial College in 1963. Roth acrimoniously left the country to join the World Bank in 1967, citing the delays and the mutation of the pricing scheme from an enabling investment-raising mechanism into a method of restriction.

It remained influential elsewhere, with economist Maurice Allais following up this work in 1965 with a report for the EEC that recommended rail and road privatisation to allow the operation of free market forces across Europe's roads and railways, and with the Adam Smith Institute who encouraged Roth to revisit his earlier analysis in 1992, when he noted that "the idea of charging for the use of congested roads is still hypersensitive, and many politicians avoid the subject studiously."

Although Singapore adopted Smeed's approach (after Roth analysed its congestion problems for the World Bank) it was not until 2002 that the principle was re-adopted in Britain, with legislation passed to allow the first schemes to be implemented in Durham and then London, with consideration given to a national road pricing system. Research by the likes of Lewis and Mogridge were better able to formulate the observation that the more roads are built, the more traffic there is to fill these roads. Combined with the visible effects of growing levels of traffic, this developed the intellectual argument upon which to consider introducing new methods of charging.

Comparison with today's schemes

Most of the features and considerations identified in the Smeed Report were consistent with those of the British congestion charging schemes implemented 40 years later.

Perhaps the biggest change relates to the method of charging and collection, as the available technologies have changed over time. Thus the Durham scheme uses an automated toll booth, while London uses a remote system based on CCTV and automatic number plate recognition.

As predicted, the costs of tracking and billing are very large; for the remote monitoring of the London scheme the majority of the income raised is absorbed by the costs. There are suggestions that a wireless "tag and beacon" scheme could be introduced as a potentially better and cheaper alternative.

There are no multiple zones in operation in the UK; when it was decided to extend congestion charging from central London to include the West End of London, there was some discussion about having two zones running side-by-side. However, the Western zone was introduced by simply extending the area of the earlier London zone and use the same charges and conditions for simplicity.

Although the more recent Data Protection Act now gives a framework for the responsible collection of personal data in the UK, the privacy concerns identified in the Smeed report were not addressed by the London scheme, with fears expressed over mass surveillance and abuse of the systems.

Edinburgh seriously considered a two-cordon road pricing scheme but rejected it in 2005 after a public referendum.

Singapore has adopted many of the ideas originally identified in the Smeed Report, since introducing its first Restricted Zone in 1975. It uses a variable Electronic Road Pricing structure on expressways and through gateways into the central business district with pricing based on time and congestion levels. It aims to reduce congestion, encourage the use of public transport, car pooling, less congested alternative routes and different times of travel. Since 1998 it has operated through a wireless In-vehicle Unit which communicates with the overhead gantries, and makes electronic payments through an electronic CashCard. A cordon based charging scheme has also been running in the city centre of Oslo, Norway since 1990. However, this differs in some key respects from Smeed's scheme, as it relies on a system of 19 wireless AutoPASS-enabled entrypoints with toll booths, and it was not designed as a congestion charge. Instead it is a hypothecated tax or fund-raising mechanism to pay for new roads, in the first instance, and public transport more latterly.

Source (edited): "http://en.wikipedia.org/wiki/Smeed_Report"

Streetcar (carsharing)

Streetcar is the United Kingdom's largest carsharing company, with over 75,000 members. Vehicles are parked in a dense network of dedicated spaces primarily in London, but also across a total of 10 UK cities including Brighton, Bristol, Cambridge, Edinburgh, Glasgow, Oxford, Guildford, Maidstone and Southampton. Members can book vehicles from 30 minutes up to six months, online or by phone. A smartcard is used to pick up and return the car at any time of the day or night, 365 days a year.

On 21 April 2010, Streetcar and Zipcar announced a merger of their rival operations. The fleets will be merged under the Zipcar brand and in-vehicle technology and will give the combined membership of both companies access to more than 1,000 vehicles around England, as well as international access to vehicles in Zipcar's existing markets across the United States, and Canada. The merger plan resulted in a request from the Office of Fair Trading for an enquiry by the British Competition Commission, which is expected to deliver its report in January 2011, as a merger would mean that the combined company would control 80-90% of the UK market.

History

A Streetcar in London.

Durham University friends Brett Akker and Andrew Valentine founded Streetcar after seeing its commercial success in the US. They started with 8 cars in locations near Clapham Junction station, and much of the growth since inception has occurred organically through word-of-mouth recommendations.

The Streetcar fleet now consists of VW Golfs, VW Polos, VW Transporter vans and VW Tourans. From January 2010, Streetcar also introduced the BMW 1 Series and BMW 3 Series to their fleet. The BMW models Streetcar chose, the 116d, 118d and 318d are all class leading cars, with carbon emissions of 119g/km and efficiency of 62.8 mpg across the range. In June 2009, Streetcar became the first UK car club to provide an electric car to its members, as part of a trial with Camden Council.

In January 2010, Streetcar also launched their own iPhone application (which is free to download), allowing members across the UK to locate, book and even open a car using their iPhone or iPod touch.

Streetcar currently has over 1,200 locations across 10 UK cities including; London, Edinburgh, Glasgow, Bristol, Cambridge, Oxford, Brighton, Southampton, Guildford, and Maidstone.

Membership details

Streetcars are booked online or by phone, and can be collected and returned at any time using the member's personal smart card and PIN. Usage charges are based on the length of time the client keeps the car, and mileage during the rental (the first 20 miles per calendar day are free). In June 2009 Streetcar announced that members would no longer have to pay London's congestion charge. For car bookings over 72 hours the cost of fuel is included (up to a fair use limit of 500 miles per week, excludes peak weekends,this doesn't apply in July and August). For bookings shorter than 72 hours, 20 miles fuel is provided per calendar day, after which additional mileage is charged at 23p per mile. On March 1st 2011, Streetcar announced that their Overnight Rate would become a permanent feature, after previously being a limited offer. With this, members can book a Streetcar or Streetvan from 6pm to 9am, Monday to Thursday, for just £25.

Membership of Streetcar costs £59.50 per year, with cars available from £5.25 per hour.

Streetcar for Business

In 2008, Streetcar launched "Streetcar for Business" as a result of its developing relationship with companies across the UK, and in recognition of the differing needs of businesses and individuals. Business accounts (which cost £99 annually) provide employees access to every vehicle in the Streetcar fleet, with the option to add drivers to the account for a one-off charge of £10 each. The service has been used as an example of a practical and green alternative to grey fleets or reimbursed private mileage.

Over 2,000 businesses are registered members of Streetcar for Business, with corporate clients of the pay-as-you-go scheme include Kellogg's, as well as local government authorities including Surrey County Council.

Streetvan

In July 2008 Streetcar launched Streetvan, in conjunction with Homebase and Big Yellow Self Storage. Streetvan membership costs £19.50 per year, and provides members with access to every van in the fleet. All vehicles are VW Transporter vans, and are available for £8.95 per hour.

Competitors

Streetcar's main competitors on the UK market are City Car Club, and in London also Streetcar's new owner Zipcar and Connect by Hertz.

Environmental and financial benefits

Membership of Car clubs such as Streetcar can make a valuable environmental contribution: Research by Transport for London shows that each Streetcar takes some 26 cars off the roads for every one club car put on the road. Research has also shown that using carsharing clubs such as Streetcar can have financial benefits. According to government-sponsored website carclubs.org.uk, car owners who drive less than 6,000 miles a year can save up to £3,500.

Source (edited): "http://en.wikipedia.org/wiki/Streetcar_(carsharing)"

Traffic in Towns

Traffic in Towns was an influential report and popular book on urban and transport planning policy produced in 1963 for the UK Department of Transport by a team headed by the architect, civil engineer and planner Professor Sir Colin Buchanan. The report warned of the potential damage caused by the motor car, while offering ways to mitigate it:

Urban roads in Bristol

"It is impossible to spend any time on the study of the future of traffic in towns without at once being appalled by the magnitude of the emergency that is coming upon us. We are nourishing at immense cost a monster of great potential destructiveness, and yet we love him dearly. To refuse to accept the challenge it presents would be an act of defeatism."

It gave planners a set of policy blueprints to deal with its effects on the urban environment, including traffic containment and segregation, which could be balanced against urban redevelopment, new corridor and distribution roads and precincts.

These policies shaped the development of the urban landscape in the UK and some other countries for two or three decades. Unusually for a technical policy report, it was so much in demand that Penguin abridged it and republished it as a book.

Background

Buchanan's report was commissioned in 1960 by Ernest Marples, Transport Minister in the Macmillan government, whose manifesto had promised to improve the existing road network and relieve congestion in the towns.

Britain was still reconstructing itself after the devastation of World War II, and, although the economy was recovering, towns and cities still had large areas of bomb damage that needed rebuilding or re-use. New motorways were being planned and built across the country, and the motor car was already starting to fill up towns and villages. Wartime had seen the establishment of central planning, and the discipline of urban planning was looking for good patterns and policies to be implemented as they rebuilt.

Although the government was looking to manage motor vehicle growth, potentially with a congestion charge as suggested by the Smeed Report, this was contrasted by a strong desire for dramatic cost-saving measures in nationalised public transport. Doctor Beeching's proposed closure of a third of the passenger railway lines, the retirement of tramways and shunning of light rail, with bus services offering a partial replacement, all emphasised the widely-held expectation that "progress" would see an increasing dependency on private motor cars. This represented a departure from the previous policies set by the Salter Report of 1933, which looked to balance the needs of railways against motor vehicles.

Predictions

New Austin Maestros waiting to be delivered

At the time of the report, there were 10.5 million vehicles registered in Britain, but, at predicted growth rates, this number was expected to become 18 m by 1970, hit 27 m by 1980 before about 40 m vehicles would be reached in 2010, or 540 vehicles for every 1000 population, equivalent to 1.3 cars per household. They expected growth in traffic to be uneven, with more congestion in the south east of England, and to incorporate a population that would reach 74 million.

The impact of the motor car was compared to a juggernaut which;

"given its head, would wreck our towns within a decade... The problems of traffic are crowding in upon us with desperate urgency. Unless steps are taken, the motor vehicle will defeat its own utility and bring about a disastrous degradation of the surroundings for living... Either the utility of vehicles in town will decline rapidly, or the pleasantness and safety of surroundings will deteriorate catastrophically – in all probability both will happen."

"Indeed it can be said in advance that the measures required to deal with the full potential amount of motor traffic in big cities are so formidable that society will have to ask itself seriously how far it is prepared to go with the motor vehicle."

There was a need to limit vehicle access to some urban areas:

"Distasteful though we find the whole idea, we think that some deliberate limitation of the volume of motor traffic is quite unavoidable. The need for it just can't be escaped. Even when everything that is possibly to do by way of building new roads and expanding public transport has been done, there would still be, in the absence of deliberate limitation, more cars trying to move into, or within our cities than could possibly be accommodated."

Already the growth of vehicle ownership in America had not been held back by congestion in urban areas; they observed that congestion in Britain's smaller land mass might limit the *use* of cars but probably not affect people's desire for ownership as they became more affluent and hoped to *try* to use their cars. They saw the day coming when most adults would take the car "as much for granted as an overcoat", and value it as an "asset of the first order".

There would also be pressure to house a growing population and disperse more population away from overcrowded cities. However, dispersing the population around the countryside would be synonymous with urban sprawl, and would defeat one of the reasons for car ownership, to get out into the countryside. Having examined the road network in Los Angeles and Fort Worth, Buchanan wished to avoid their dehumanising effects and their creation of pedestrian "no-go" areas. He also wished to ensure that the heritage within British towns was respected:

"The American policy of providing motorways for commuters can succeed, even in American conditions, only if there is a disregard for all considerations other than the free flow of traffic which seems sometimes to be almost ruthless. Our British cities are not only packed with buildings, they are also packed with history and to drive motorways through them on the American scale would inevitably destroy much that ought to be preserved."

The rise of traffic congestion would waste people's time, who would soon have to spend time sitting in traffic, in addition to their time spent in sleep, work, and leisure. Already, the average speed in many cities had fallen to 11 mph, and congestion was costing the British economy £250 m in wasted manhours.

Yet the motor car was also inextricably linked to the economy, with 2,305,000 people working in the motor trade, or ten percent of the labour force. It had already eclipsed the railway, and would become more prominent in the movement of goods and the workforce. The expansion of public transport would not provide an answer on its own.

However, the noise, fumes, pollution and visual intrusion of the cars and ugly traffic paraphernalia would overwhelm town centres, while vehicles parked on streets would force new hazards onto children at play.

Safety considerations should move to become foremost in the design of streets; three quarters of all injury accidents were occurring within towns (although most fatalities happened on open roads). They feared that future generations would think that they were careless and callous to mix people and moving vehicles on the same streets.

The report warned of trying to find a single "solution":
"We have found it desirable to avoid the term 'solution' altogether for the traffic problem is not such much a problem waiting for a solution as a social situation requiring to be dealt with by policies patiently applied over a period and revised from time to time in light of events"

Recommendations

Gracechurch Shopping Centre, Sutton Coldfield, Birmingham. An example of the new style of 1960-70's pedestrian precinct, separated from the historic road network, but at the cost of demolition of the earlier town Parade

The report signified some fundamental shifts in attitudes to roads, by recognising that there were environmental disbenefits from traffic, and that large increases in capacity can exacerbate congestion problems, not solve them. This awareness of environmental impact was ahead of its time, and not translated into policy for some years in other countries, such as Germany or the USA, where the promotion of traffic flow remained paramount The scale of traffic growth envisaged would soon overtake any benefits that small scale road improvement would offer, which would anyway divert attention from the large scale solutions that would be needed. These solutions would be very expensive and could only be justified if they were comprehensively planned, including social as well as traffic needs. However, the report saw no turning back from people's new-found dependence on the car, and thought that there would be limits to how much traffic could be transferred to railways and buses.

Towns should be worth living in, which meant more than just the ability to drive into the centre. Urban redevelopment should look to the long term, and avoid parsimonious short-termism. The report asked how bold the planners could be, when restricting access to town centres and controlling traffic flows:
"It is a difficult and dangerous thing in a democracy to prevent a substantial part of the population from doing things they do not regard as wrong. ... The freedom with which a person can walk about and look around is a very useful guide to the civilized quality of an urban area ... judged against this standard, many of our towns now seem to leave a great deal to be desired ... there must be areas of good environment where people can live, work, shop, look about and move around on foot in reasonable freedom from the hazards of motor traffic."
The report recommended that certain standards should always be met, including safety, visual intrusion, noise, and pollution limits. But if a city was both financially able and willing, it should rebuild itself with modern traffic in mind. However, if circumstances meant that this was not possible it would have to restrain traffic, perhaps severely.

This was revolutionary and ran counter to the wisdom of economists, who assumed that environmental standards could be set off against other considerations once they had been priced.

Planners should set a policy regarding the character being sought for each urban area, and the level of traffic should then be managed to produced the desired effect, in a safe manner. This would result in towns with a lattice of environmentally-planned areas joined by a road hierarchy, a network of distribution roads, with longer-distance traffic being directed around and away from these areas, rather like an interior would be designed with corridors serving a multitude of rooms.

It recommended the selective use of bypasses around small and medium sized towns to alleviate congestion in the centres, even though local businesses might complain at the loss of through-trade; the predicted increase in traffic would become more than an unmitigated nuisance in the future. However, it rejected a slavish use of ring-roads around large towns. As the detailed plans of these schemes often demanded far more land for junctions and wide roads than would be acceptable, it would be better to place restrictions on the volume of traffic that could access the area in these cases.

Where restrictions were needed, this could often be achieved through some combination of licences or permits, parking restrictions, or subsidised public transport. However it recommended that the road user should not be denied too much access, and that restricting through congestion charging would not normally be the right approach, unless and until every possible alternative had been tested:
"We think the public can justifiably demand to be fully informed about the possibilities of adapting towns to motor traffic before there is any question of applying restrictive measures."

Above ground multi-storey car park near Kilmarnock centre, one (visually intrusive) solution to the problem of accommodating cars next to retail redevelopment

Innovatively, the report recommended that some areas should change their outlook; rather than facing onto the street, shops could face onto squares or pedestrianised streets, with roof top or multi-storey parking nearby. Urban areas need not consist of buildings set alongside vehicular streets, instead multiple levels could be used with traffic moving underneath a building deck, with snug pedestrian alleys and contrasting open squares containing fountains and artwork.

Schemes would need to be carefully considered when they incorporated historic buildings, but such schemes could not be applied to small areas. However, obsolete street patterns were already becoming frozen for decades by piecemeal rebuilding. Whilst these grand schemes would be expensive, the income from vehicle taxes could represent a regular source of income to draw from.

This approach differed from the shopping mall concept, which was designed for the car on greenfield or out of town sites, and did not address the development of the existing urban landscape.

Examples

The report looked at a range of scenarios based on real towns, and suggested treatments that would balance the desire to enrich people's lives through car ownership while still maintain pleasant urban centres.

London (Oxford Street area)

Oxford Street, in London's West End "epitomizes the conflict between traffic and environment". The mixing of traffic and pedestrians had created "the most uncivilised street in Europe". The report had considered running car parks, through-traffic and access roads in shallow cuttings underground while raising the shop levels over four pedestrianised storeys 20 feet above it. However they concluded that this had already become impractical – for a generation at least – because of piecemeal redevelopment. Should this practice continue, the only choice would be to ultimately curtail vehicular access to the street.

Leeds - A large city

pedestrianised shopping centre

Urban dual carriageways

Leeds, as a large city, was too large to accommodate all the potential traffic, and it should instead attempt to curtail access, particularly private vehicles being used for commuting. Leeds embraced the approach and adopted the motto *Motorway city of the 70s* after it built an Outer Ring Road, a sunken part-motorway Inner Ring Road and a clockwise-only 'loop road' enclosing a part-pedestrianised city centre with several business and shopping centres. The protection and redevelopment of the city centre came at the cost of the large landtake required for the network of corridor roads and interchanges, predominantly at ground level, which required extensive demolition and severed the previous urban and suburban communities.

Newbury - a small town

Newbury was chosen as an example of a small town that could be redeveloped following this pattern, with vehicles easily integrating into the urban scenery. But the report warned that the commitment and scale of work required would be hitherto unheard of. The concept was mainly ignored for 25 years until the A34 Newbury bypass was proposed, alongside extensive pedestrianisation and road changes within the urban areas. The new roads dramatically reduced the impact of motor vehicles on the town, especially heavy goods vehicles, and accompanied the reinvigoration of Newbury which had managed to retain its historic core. When completed in 1998 the actual bypass followed approximately the same route as the original proposal, but encountered such protest from so many quarters that all other UK road schemes were soon stalled. As a result the government and Highways Agency changed its policies and assessment criteria to evenly balance predictions of schemes' environmental impact with their economic, community and safety benefits

Norwich - an ancient town

Norwich, as an ancient town, could retain its historic areas but this would be at the cost of reduced vehicular access.

Response and legacy

The RAC recognised that some conclusions were unpalatable, and controversial, but overall they welcomed the approach. However, they thought that restrictions on vehicular traffic would be acceptable to the motorist if they could see the government determined to build capacity in urban areas. The Pedestrian Association cautioned that "the Judgment of Solomon" would be needed to decide how to implement the ideas in the report.

The Parliamentary transport committee welcomed the report, as it offered an alternative to simply building more roads or providing more public transport. Thus it gained political currency, with the report forming the blueprint for UK urban planning for the next few decades.

In doing so, it gave acceptability and confidence to a number of proposals and innovations that soon became common in the UK landscape:

- urban clearways, flyovers, and the widespread used of single and double yellow lines to limit the intrusion of vehicles in town centres
- pedestrianised precincts
- pedestrian city centres flanked with multi-storey car parks
- one way streets and traffic restrictions
- separation of pedestrians and traffic, with clearly defined kerbs and pedestrian barriers

Buchanan later proposed a development for Bath using the same approach to reduce traffic in the historical city centre by way of underground routes; this provoked such a storm of local protest that "Buchanan's Tunnel" was never built.

The recognition that road congestion could not be addressed just through new road programmes influenced the way that traffic problems would be addressed in future; there would now be a switch towards "transport studies" which should consider multi-modal solutions, i.e. both road and public transport options, including park and ride. However, in the absence of a central commitment to public transport the perspective was skewed in favour of road building for many years to come. By 1970 the government had committed to spend £4 bn on road schemes to "eliminate congestion" over the next 15 years.

However, this switch to a multi-modal approach took some time to become widely accepted, and meanwhile many grand road schemes were being planned. By 1970 there were plans to spend £1,700 million on multiple Ringways and elevated radial roads across London. Robert Vigars, the chairman of the Greater London Council's Planning committee, reported that the plan for a part-buried Ringway 2 to supersede the South Circular Road between the A2 and A23 would necessitate the destruction of several thousand houses, but it was:

"not just a traffic solution but a plan for the very people whose areas it passes through. It means creating living standards for them, so that they can live, breathe, shop and eat free from the menace of traffic congestion in their local streets. This was putting Buchanan into action ... We are satisfied that the total planning and environmental gains greatly outweigh the local difficulties."

Criticisms

As towns were developed according to the Buchanan blueprint, several issues emerged.

- Some of the grand plans that were called for have had a poor reputation in their implementation; to be able to predict future trends, mix social development, transport skills, and economic regeneration while performing slum clearance has often been beyond the capability of the local planners. Public accountability required by local government officers was sometimes stretched, with accusations of corruption with the private sector developers and contractors who put the plans into action. The cost inflation of schemes conspired with fluctuation of the property market and its subsequent collapse in the early 1970s left many plans incomplete. When conditions had improved conservation had once again become fashionable and confidence in the need for these centrally-controlled grand plans had evaporated.

Uncompleted Motorway Junction on the M23 towards London. Work stopped in the 1970s

- The courage needed to develop these schemes required a lot of political will, and this would sometimes falter. By failing to identify cheaper alternatives when the financial case weakened, "do-nothing" often became the default action. For example, the extensive plans to develop a series of orbital and distribution roads into central London resulted in the construction of the A40(M) Westway, the M41 cross route and A102(M) Blackwall tunnel. However, the wide impact of these schemes raised such controversy during the 1970s that many associated road schemes soon ran into concerted opposition. After the 1973 oil crisis, those remaining schemes fell into limbo, casting a planning blight over the affected areas for a decade or more until they were finally laid to rest. The recognition of environmental issues was also less well understood in the 1960s; the report's considerations were more for the human environment, rather than the natural issues which have tended to confound some subsequent road proposals.
- More latterly, this policy has been accused as being one of "predict and provide", or of building new roads in a congested network that fuel demand for more traffic, rather than meeting previous demands. This is to partly misrepresent the policy

recommendations; although neither traffic generation and the deterrent effect of congestion, nor the mechanisms by which a business would choose to (re-)locate his premises was understood at the time, the report strove to strike a balance for situations when capacity demands could not or should not be met. Radical urban surgery was almost the opposite of what Buchanan was proposing, he later claimed:

"in spite of all the effort, it was widely misinterpreted ... the Report was a description of the choices open, from 'do nothing to whole hog', with the advantages and disadvantages set out."

- The separation of road users would often be taken to extremes in schemes: by moving motor vehicles onto dedicated routes, their interaction with pedestrians or cycle routes might occur less often but at higher speeds than before, and thus be far more hazardous or intimidating. New towns like Milton Keynes could avoid this by placing motorists, cyclists, and pedestrians on separate levels and routes. However, their interaction would be a particular problem in the established towns, especially in the transition to suburban areas where separation would be more ambiguous and inconsistent. In the search for low casualty rates, urban planners now look to detailed road designs and traffic calming to counteract this affect by reducing vehicle speeds, or take more dramatic steps by destroying this separation and mixing all road users together through shared space planning.
- At the heart of many of the new schemes was architecture of poor quality or poor design, and a poor understanding of the effects of the new road network. As warned by Buchanan, the detailed implementation of many of these schemes critically affected their success or failure. Subsequent research has shown that more is needed than a pedestrian centre with glass shop fronts and a hope that people will come and social life flourish. One of the recommendations, that of integrating low level roads with developments on top, has been largely ignored; the costs and commitments needed for multi-level developments have been prohibitive in old town centres, especially when cheaper alternatives or out of town sites have presented themselves. New developments were often made in a fashionable modernist or brutalist style which rapidly dated, while the planners had not fully considered the social or economic factors that could lead to urban decay. The corridor or distribution roads would often have minimal overpasses or grade separation, with communities severed or blighted by noise and fumes. Drivers would refuse to be neatly compartmentalised into "travelling" along the corridor roads and "living" on the local roads, leading to businesses closing outside the prime sites.
- Actual traffic growth has not been as extreme as envisaged in the report (although Buchanan did warn that he had selecting the more pessimistic projections). In 1963 36% of households had a car, by 1998 this had grown to 72%, considerably less than predicted. This pattern of inaccuracy was a frequent issue with early transport schemes, which frequently over-estimated vehicle ownership by about 20%, leading to a suspicion that they were often motivated by a feeling that they were important for "modernisation" for their own sake.

Influences

Darlington, a modern interpretation of a pedestrian centre with restricted car access

The design of modern town schemes has been informed by the earlier policy decisions – and mistakes – in Britain, Europe and further afield. Auckland, for example, commissioned a plan from Buchanan for its road policies.

By the mid 1970s it was evident that the previous focus on road traffic element was not enough; transport schemes were forced to widen the study area to include land use changes, and the effects of public transport, which continued to decline in popularity. This came to a head in 1976 when Nottingham rejected plans for new urban highways in favour of another (later also rejected) scheme to place access restrictions on cars entering the city centre. Instead, authorities' efforts were put to work improving the forecasting models, adjust local traffic management to squeeze more out of the current road system, directing heavy lorries away from minor roads, or subsidising public transport, which was now carrying fewer passengers and becoming uneconomic. The roads programme was scaled back to half its previous size mainly because of poor public finances, and urban regeneration became much more locally driven through "Strategic Plans". Although many public policies and transport planners have promoted the creation of capacity-oriented solutions, organisations such as The Urban Motorways Committee (1972) adopted the need to respect the urban fabric. This movement has developed into a recognition of the need to effectively manage the demand for transport.

Subsequent government planning policy on sustainable development adopted as consequence of the 1992 Earth Summit means that the concepts of vehicle restriction first mooted by Buchanan are slowly moving to the forefront of UK government policy. This has placed emphasis on alternatives to the private motor car, but has also embraced other techniques of restriction. Smeed's report of 1964 had proposed congestion charging as technically feasible, although Buchanan's recommendation had largely dismissed it. It took four decades for it to become politically acceptable in the UK, although this was not without controversy.

Buchanan's concept of segregated zones or precincts, as pedestrian or local vehiclar areas, was derived from Assistant Commissioner H. Alker Tripp of Scotland Yard's Traffic Division. Buchanan's articulation of this concept encouraged the planners of the Dutch towns of Emmen and Delft, who were developing the concept of the woonerf, or living street, and decades later this was fed back to Britain, as the "home zone".

Cities in the USA slowly came round to respond to the problems that Buchanan identified in 1963. A notable example is the elevated freeway system built in the late 1950s to provide extra capacity for Boston's traffic, which, at enormous financial cost, was demolished and rebuilt underground many decades later thus creating road capacity, urban pedestrian space, and reuniting displaced communities.
Source (edited): "http://en.wikipedia.org/wiki/Traffic_in_Towns"

Victoria Coach Station

Victoria Coach Station is the largest and most significant coach station in London. It serves long distance coach services and is also the departure point for many countryside coach tours originating from London. It should not be confused with the nearby Green Line Coach Station serving Green Line Coaches, Greyhound UK or the Victoria bus station, which serves London Buses. It is operated by Victoria Coach Station Ltd which is a part of Transport for London.

History

Victoria Coach Station was opened at its present site in Buckingham Palace Road, London, in 1932, by London Coastal Coaches Limited, an association of coach operators. The building is in a distinctive Art Deco style, the architects for which were Wallis, Gilbert and Partners.

It was originally managed by London Coastal Coaches Limited, a consortium of coach operators. In 1970 it became a subsidiary of the National Bus Company (UK) (NBC).

During the 1970s, Victoria Coach Station became the responsibility of the NBC subsidiary, National Travel (South East) Limited. In 1978, London Coastal Coaches Company was brought back to life and renamed Victoria Coach Station Limited.

In the 1990s major work was carried out:
- Victoria Coach Station Departures Terminal (1990–1992) £4.1m
- Victoria Coach Station Arrivals Garage (1991) £500K
- Victoria Coach Station Arrivals Terminal (1993–1994) £330K

In 1988, following the privatisation of the NBC companies, ownership of Victoria Coach Station Limited was transferred to London Transport. In 2000 ownership passed to Transport for London.

In 2008 works were carried on the roof, the toilets and staff facilities costing £320K.

Operation

Victoria Coach Station arrivals and departures terminals, located on the opposite sides of Elizabeth Street. The main departures building includes food outlets, shops, left luggage facilities and ticketing. The coach station accommodates mostly National Express, Eurolines, Oxford Espress and Megabus.

There are 21 departure gates and 26 coach bays and the site covers 3.3 acres (13,000 m). 10 million passengers use the station every year with services to 1,200 destinations in the UK and 400 in mainland Europe.

Gallery

Victoria Coach Station, exterior

Gates 1-9

A National Express coach on route A6 at Victoria Coach Station.
Source (edited): "http://en.wikipedia.org/wiki/Victoria_Coach_Station"

Westminster motorcycle parking charge

The **Westminster motorcycle parking charge** is a charge that Westminster Council makes for parking motorcycles in designated on-street and off-street motorcycle parking bays in the City of Westminster. It was introduced in August 2008 as an Experimental Order made under the authority of the Road Traffic Regulation Act 1984. Experimental Orders may not, under the Act, last for more than 18 months, but do not require the formal advertisement and objection procedures of permanent Traffic Regulation Orders (TROs) made under the Act. In June 2009, Westminster Council gave notice that it was to turn this into a permanent Traffic Regulation Order.

The Council stated that its reason for introducing the charge was that, as a consequence of the introduction of the London congestion charge in 2003, many more people had taken to riding motorcycles into the City of Westminster. 2008 figures stated that 16,000 motorcyclists rode into London every day, a rise of 40% in 10 years. Before introducing the Experimental Order, the council increased the number of motorcycle parking bays from 4,500 to 6,400 (6,150 on-street and 400 off-street). However, having previously stopped motorcyclists parking on pavements and waste land, the overall parking spaces available were in fact reduced. Initially, the charge was £1.50 per diem per motorcycle, with discounted rates for longer periods (£5 per week; £20 per month; £50 per quarter; and £150 per annum).

The permanent TRO differed from the Experimental Order in three major respects. Residents were allowed to park in designated motorcycle parking bays free of charge as long as they displayed a valid residents permit; parking in all of the off-street motorcycle parking bays was made free of charge; and the scale of charges was reduced. The new scale of charges was £1 per diem per motorcycle, with discounted rates for longer periods (£3.50 per week; £13.50 per month; £33.50 per quarter; and £100 per annum).

Prior to the Experimental Order in 2007, the Council had consulted with several interest groups, including the British Motorcyclists Federation (BMF). The BMF had campaigned against the charge, but in 2008 at the time of the issuance of the Experimental Order a spokesman reported that the Federation's members "on balance" thought that the deal of paying for parking spaces was "not a bad one", since motorcyclists didn't have to pay the London congestion charge and had lower running costs, even though the BMF members didn't like charges.

Subsequent to the Experimental Order, the formal protest group No To Bike Parking Tax was formed to oppose the measures. It presented formal objections to the Council's Built Environmental Policy and Scrutiny Committee on 2009-03-31. It also organized several public protests, including "go-slows" where motorcyclists rode slowly through central London during peak "rush hour" traffic times causing road closures and traffic problems, in December 2008 and March 2009.

On Wednesday 2010-04-16, local councillor Daniel Hamilton (for the Englefield Green East ward of the borough of Runnymede), having had his journey to work delayed by half an hour by a No To Bike Parking Tax rush-hour "go slow", called the demonstrators "tossers" on his Twitter account. In response, he received 200 electronic mail messages, numerous text messages and telephone calls, including 15 death threats. In June 2010, Boris Johnson was caught up in the protests and was heard to make what appeared to be veiled threats . In March 2009, Westminster councillors responded to what they perceived to be a "hate campaign" organized by protesters, where councillors' names, addresses, and telephone numbers had been posted on the Internet, alongside threatening statements that people who supported the parking charge "must accept the consequences of their actions" and statements calling for "total war" against staff at the Council. Throughout, the Council maintained its position that the parking charges were necessary in order to meet the increased demand for motorcycle parking and would not be abolished. The campaigners maintained their opposition to the scheme, describing the councillors as "arrogant" and dismissing the charges that there was a "hate campaign" as an attempt to distract from the issue of the charge itself. The Council held that it was right that motorcyclists contributed towards road maintenance through the payment of a parking charge, and protesters countered that many motorcyclists could not afford the charge imposed.

Some 4,000 motorcyclists turned out for a demonstration ride through central London. Being ignored by Westminster council, as well as being accused of "polluting more than a Hummer SUV" upset bikers even further. Since then, an allied group, the NoToMob has regained much public support by introducing $CAMera car hunting aka schunting. This involves volunteers in hi-vis clothing drawing attention to the CCTV equipped enforcement cars, which are often parked stealthily, and to unclear prohibition signs so motorists do not commit offences. This keeps the roads safer and helps achieve the stated goal of "100% compliance without penalties" by making the CCTV cars the "visible deterrent" they are claimed to be.

The No To Bike Parking Tax campaigners took the issue to the High Court, arguing that the parking charge was simply a device to raise revenue, and that proper consultation, in line with the Road Traffic Regulation Act, had not been undertaken by the Council. By 2009, revenue that Westminster Council was obtaining from parking charges in general, some £81.5 millions per annum from parking meters and parking fines, had already exceeded the £80 millions per annum revenue that it was obtaining from council tax. Councillor Danny Chalkley, the Council's cabinet member for city management, had stated then that no profit was made from parking charges, and that all surpluses (£35 millions in 2008) were invested in the Council's transport projects. Many of the protesters had already asserted, via electronic mail to councillors, letters, and petitions with more than 3,000 signatures, that the Council was using the charge simply to raise revenue. By February 2009, the cost to the Council of creating the extra motorcycle parking bays and the additional security measures, some £300,000, had been exceeded by the £2.2 millions that the Council had obtained from parking charges and fines. The High Court ruled against the campaigners on both counts in July 2010. Lord Justice Pitchford, who heard the case alongside Mr Justice Maddison, stated that the scheme had not been invalidated by Westminster Council budgeting for a modest surplus, nor did that mean that there was an ulterior motive in charging motorcyclists. The Council stated, after the ruling, that it was seeking reimbursement of its £50,000 legal fees from Warren Djanogly, chairman of the NTBPT campaign, whose own legal fees were already estimated to be £70,000.

Source (edited): "http://en.wikipedia.org/wiki/Westminster_motorcycle_parking_charge"